# This book belongs to:

_______________

Date:

_______________

© Prettyprints

Website:

Username:                                          Email:

Password:

Security Question 1:

Security Answer 1:

Security Question 2:

Security Answer 2:

Notes:


Website:

Username:                                          Email:

Password:

Security Question 1:

Security Answer 1:

Security Question 2:

Security Answer 2:

Notes:


Website:

Username:                                          Email:

Password:

Security Question 1:

Security Answer 1:

Security Question 2:

Security Answer 2:

Notes:

**Website:**

Username:                                   Email:

Password:

Security Question 1:

Security Answer 1:

Security Question 2:

Security Answer 2:

Notes:

**Website:**

Username:                                   Email:

Password:

Security Question 1:

Security Answer 1:

Security Question 2:

Security Answer 2:

Notes:

**Website:**

Username:                                   Email:

Password:

Security Question 1:

Security Answer 1:

Security Question 2:

Security Answer 2:

Notes:

## Website:

Username: Email:

Password:

Security Question 1:

Security Answer 1:

Security Question 2:

Security Answer 2:

Notes:

## Website:

Username: Email:

Password:

Security Question 1:

Security Answer 1:

Security Question 2:

Security Answer 2:

Notes:

## Website:

Username: Email:

Password:

Security Question 1:

Security Answer 1:

Security Question 2:

Security Answer 2:

Notes:

Website:

Username:                          Email:

Password:

Security Question 1:

Security Answer 1:

Security Question 2:

Security Answer 2:

Notes:


Website:

Username:                          Email:

Password:

Security Question 1:

Security Answer 1:

Security Question 2:

Security Answer 2:

Notes:


Website:

Username:                          Email:

Password:

Security Question 1:

Security Answer 1:

Security Question 2:

Security Answer 2:

Notes:

## A


Website:

Username:                    Email:

Password:

Security Question 1:

Security Answer 1:

Security Question 2:

Security Answer 2:

Notes:

Website:

Username:                    Email:

Password:

Security Question 1:

Security Answer 1:

Security Question 2:

Security Answer 2:

Notes:

Website:

Username:                    Email:

Password:

Security Question 1:

Security Answer 1:

Security Question 2:

Security Answer 2:

Notes:

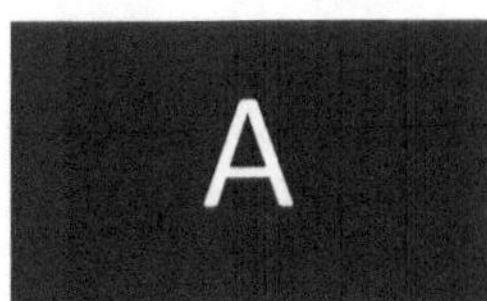


**Website:**

Username:                                   Email:

Password:

Security Question 1:

Security Answer 1:

Security Question 2:

Security Answer 2:

Notes:

**Website:**

Username:                                   Email:

Password:

Security Question 1:

Security Answer 1:

Security Question 2:

Security Answer 2:

Notes:

**Website:**

Username:                                   Email:

Password:

Security Question 1:

Security Answer 1:

Security Question 2:

Security Answer 2:

Notes:

## Website:

| | |
|---|---|
| Username: | Email: |

Password:

Security Question 1:

Security Answer 1:

Security Question 2:

Security Answer 2:

Notes:

## Website:

| | |
|---|---|
| Username: | Email: |

Password:

Security Question 1:

Security Answer 1:

Security Question 2:

Security Answer 2:

Notes:

## Website:

| | |
|---|---|
| Username: | Email: |

Password:

Security Question 1:

Security Answer 1:

Security Question 2:

Security Answer 2:

Notes:

**Website:**

Username:         Email:

Password:

Security Question 1:

Security Answer 1:

Security Question 2:

Security Answer 2:

Notes:

**Website:**

Username:         Email:

Password:

Security Question 1:

Security Answer 1:

Security Question 2:

Security Answer 2:

Notes:

**Website:**

Username:         Email:

Password:

Security Question 1:

Security Answer 1:

Security Question 2:

Security Answer 2:

Notes:

# B

Website:

Username:      Email:

Password:

Security Question 1:

Security Answer 1:

Security Question 2:

Security Answer 2:

Notes:

Website:

Username:      Email:

Password:

Security Question 1:

Security Answer 1:

Security Question 2:

Security Answer 2:

Notes:

Website:

Username:      Email:

Password:

Security Question 1:

Security Answer 1:

Security Question 2:

Security Answer 2:

Notes:

# B

**Website:**

Username:                    Email:

Password:

Security Question 1:

Security Answer 1:

Security Question 2:

Security Answer 2:

Notes:

**Website:**

Username:                    Email:

Password:

Security Question 1:

Security Answer 1:

Security Question 2:

Security Answer 2:

Notes:

**Website:**

Username:                    Email:

Password:

Security Question 1:

Security Answer 1:

Security Question 2:

Security Answer 2:

Notes:

**Website:**

Username: ___________________ Email: ___________________

Password: ___________________

Security Question 1: ___________________

Security Answer 1: ___________________

Security Question 2: ___________________

Security Answer 2: ___________________

Notes: ___________________

**Website:**

Username: ___________________ Email: ___________________

Password: ___________________

Security Question 1: ___________________

Security Answer 1: ___________________

Security Question 2: ___________________

Security Answer 2: ___________________

Notes: ___________________

**Website:**

Username: ___________________ Email: ___________________

Password: ___________________

Security Question 1: ___________________

Security Answer 1: ___________________

Security Question 2: ___________________

Security Answer 2: ___________________

Notes: ___________________

## B

Website:

Username: | Email:

Password:

Security Question 1:

Security Answer 1:

Security Question 2:

Security Answer 2:

Notes:


Website:

Username: | Email:

Password:

Security Question 1:

Security Answer 1:

Security Question 2:

Security Answer 2:

Notes:


Website:

Username: | Email:

Password:

Security Question 1:

Security Answer 1:

Security Question 2:

Security Answer 2:

Notes:

Website:

Username:                                    Email:

Password:

Security Question 1:

Security Answer 1:

Security Question 2:

Security Answer 2:

Notes:

Website:

Username:                                    Email:

Password:

Security Question 1:

Security Answer 1:

Security Question 2:

Security Answer 2:

Notes:

Website:

Username:                                    Email:

Password:

Security Question 1:

Security Answer 1:

Security Question 2:

Security Answer 2:

Notes:

**Website:**

Username:                                          Email:

Password:

Security Question 1:

Security Answer 1:

Security Question 2:

Security Answer 2:

Notes:

**Website:**

Username:                                          Email:

Password:

Security Question 1:

Security Answer 1:

Security Question 2:

Security Answer 2:

Notes:

**Website:**

Username:                                          Email:

Password:

Security Question 1:

Security Answer 1:

Security Question 2:

Security Answer 2:

Notes:

## Website:

| | |
|---|---|
| Username: | Email: |

Password:

Security Question 1:

Security Answer 1:

Security Question 2:

Security Answer 2:

Notes:

## Website:

| | |
|---|---|
| Username: | Email: |

Password:

Security Question 1:

Security Answer 1:

Security Question 2:

Security Answer 2:

Notes:

## Website:

| | |
|---|---|
| Username: | Email: |

Password:

Security Question 1:

Security Answer 1:

Security Question 2:

Security Answer 2:

Notes:

**Website:**

Username:      Email:

Password:

Security Question 1:

Security Answer 1:

Security Question 2:

Security Answer 2:

Notes:

---

**Website:**

Username:      Email:

Password:

Security Question 1:

Security Answer 1:

Security Question 2:

Security Answer 2:

Notes:

---

**Website:**

Username:      Email:

Password:

Security Question 1:

Security Answer 1:

Security Question 2:

Security Answer 2:

Notes:

**Website:**

Username:      Email:

Password:

Security Question 1:

Security Answer 1:

Security Question 2:

Security Answer 2:

Notes:

**Website:**

Username:      Email:

Password:

Security Question 1:

Security Answer 1:

Security Question 2:

Security Answer 2:

Notes:

**Website:**

Username:      Email:

Password:

Security Question 1:

Security Answer 1:

Security Question 2:

Security Answer 2:

Notes:

Website:

Username: | Email:

Password:

Security Question 1:

Security Answer 1:

Security Question 2:

Security Answer 2:

Notes:

Website:

Username: | Email:

Password:

Security Question 1:

Security Answer 1:

Security Question 2:

Security Answer 2:

Notes:

Website:

Username: | Email:

Password:

Security Question 1:

Security Answer 1:

Security Question 2:

Security Answer 2:

Notes:

## Website:

Username:                                          Email:

Password:

Security Question 1:

Security Answer 1:

Security Question 2:

Security Answer 2:

Notes:

## Website:

Username:                                          Email:

Password:

Security Question 1:

Security Answer 1:

Security Question 2:

Security Answer 2:

Notes:

## Website:

Username:                                          Email:

Password:

Security Question 1:

Security Answer 1:

Security Question 2:

Security Answer 2:

Notes:

**Website:**

Username: Email:

Password:

Security Question 1:

Security Answer 1:

Security Question 2:

Security Answer 2:

Notes:

**Website:**

Username: Email:

Password:

Security Question 1:

Security Answer 1:

Security Question 2:

Security Answer 2:

Notes:

**Website:**

Username: Email:

Password:

Security Question 1:

Security Answer 1:

Security Question 2:

Security Answer 2:

Notes:

Website:

Username:                                    Email:

Password:

Security Question 1:

Security Answer 1:

Security Question 2:

Security Answer 2:

Notes:


Website:

Username:                                    Email:

Password:

Security Question 1:

Security Answer 1:

Security Question 2:

Security Answer 2:

Notes:


Website:

Username:                                    Email:

Password:

Security Question 1:

Security Answer 1:

Security Question 2:

Security Answer 2:

Notes:

Website:

Username:                                          Email:

Password:

Security Question 1:

Security Answer 1:

Security Question 2:

Security Answer 2:

Notes:


Website:

Username:                                          Email:

Password:

Security Question 1:

Security Answer 1:

Security Question 2:

Security Answer 2:

Notes:


Website:

Username:                                          Email:

Password:

Security Question 1:

Security Answer 1:

Security Question 2:

Security Answer 2:

Notes:

D

Website:

Username:                                          Email:

Password:

Security Question 1:

Security Answer 1:

Security Question 2:

Security Answer 2:

Notes:

Website:

Username:                                          Email:

Password:

Security Question 1:

Security Answer 1:

Security Question 2:

Security Answer 2:

Notes:

Website:

Username:                                          Email:

Password:

Security Question 1:

Security Answer 1:

Security Question 2:

Security Answer 2:

Notes:

## Website:

Username: _______________ Email: _______________

Password: _______________

Security Question 1: _______________

Security Answer 1: _______________

Security Question 2: _______________

Security Answer 2: _______________

Notes: _______________

## Website:

Username: _______________ Email: _______________

Password: _______________

Security Question 1: _______________

Security Answer 1: _______________

Security Question 2: _______________

Security Answer 2: _______________

Notes: _______________

## Website:

Username: _______________ Email: _______________

Password: _______________

Security Question 1: _______________

Security Answer 1: _______________

Security Question 2: _______________

Security Answer 2: _______________

Notes: _______________

Website:

Username:        Email:

Password:

Security Question 1:

Security Answer 1:

Security Question 2:

Security Answer 2:

Notes:

Website:

Username:        Email:

Password:

Security Question 1:

Security Answer 1:

Security Question 2:

Security Answer 2:

Notes:

Website:

Username:        Email:

Password:

Security Question 1:

Security Answer 1:

Security Question 2:

Security Answer 2:

Notes:

**Website:**

Username: _______________   Email: _______________

Password: _______________

Security Question 1: _______________

Security Answer 1: _______________

Security Question 2: _______________

Security Answer 2: _______________

Notes: _______________

**Website:**

Username: _______________   Email: _______________

Password: _______________

Security Question 1: _______________

Security Answer 1: _______________

Security Question 2: _______________

Security Answer 2: _______________

Notes: _______________

**Website:**

Username: _______________   Email: _______________

Password: _______________

Security Question 1: _______________

Security Answer 1: _______________

Security Question 2: _______________

Security Answer 2: _______________

Notes: _______________

E

**Website:**

Username: ___________________  Email: ___________________

Password: ___________________

Security Question 1: ___________________

Security Answer 1: ___________________

Security Question 2: ___________________

Security Answer 2: ___________________

Notes: ___________________

**Website:**

Username: ___________________  Email: ___________________

Password: ___________________

Security Question 1: ___________________

Security Answer 1: ___________________

Security Question 2: ___________________

Security Answer 2: ___________________

Notes: ___________________

**Website:**

Username: ___________________  Email: ___________________

Password: ___________________

Security Question 1: ___________________

Security Answer 1: ___________________

Security Question 2: ___________________

Security Answer 2: ___________________

Notes: ___________________

E

**Website:**

Username: ___________________  Email: ___________________

Password: ___________________

Security Question 1: ___________________

Security Answer 1: ___________________

Security Question 2: ___________________

Security Answer 2: ___________________

Notes: ___________________

**Website:**

Username: ___________________  Email: ___________________

Password: ___________________

Security Question 1: ___________________

Security Answer 1: ___________________

Security Question 2: ___________________

Security Answer 2: ___________________

Notes: ___________________

**Website:**

Username: ___________________  Email: ___________________

Password: ___________________

Security Question 1: ___________________

Security Answer 1: ___________________

Security Question 2: ___________________

Security Answer 2: ___________________

Notes: ___________________

Website:

Username:                                    Email:

Password:

Security Question 1:

Security Answer 1:

Security Question 2:

Security Answer 2:

Notes:


Website:

Username:                                    Email:

Password:

Security Question 1:

Security Answer 1:

Security Question 2:

Security Answer 2:

Notes:


Website:

Username:                                    Email:

Password:

Security Question 1:

Security Answer 1:

Security Question 2:

Security Answer 2:

Notes:

**Website:**

Username: _______________ Email: _______________

Password: _______________

Security Question 1: _______________

Security Answer 1: _______________

Security Question 2: _______________

Security Answer 2: _______________

Notes: _______________

**Website:**

Username: _______________ Email: _______________

Password: _______________

Security Question 1: _______________

Security Answer 1: _______________

Security Question 2: _______________

Security Answer 2: _______________

Notes: _______________

**Website:**

Username: _______________ Email: _______________

Password: _______________

Security Question 1: _______________

Security Answer 1: _______________

Security Question 2: _______________

Security Answer 2: _______________

Notes: _______________

## Website:

| | |
|---|---|
| Username: | Email: |

Password:

Security Question 1:

Security Answer 1:

Security Question 2:

Security Answer 2:

Notes:

## Website:

| | |
|---|---|
| Username: | Email: |

Password:

Security Question 1:

Security Answer 1:

Security Question 2:

Security Answer 2:

Notes:

## Website:

| | |
|---|---|
| Username: | Email: |

Password:

Security Question 1:

Security Answer 1:

Security Question 2:

Security Answer 2:

Notes:

**Website:**

Username:                                      Email:

Password:

Security Question 1:

Security Answer 1:

Security Question 2:

Security Answer 2:

Notes:

**Website:**

Username:                                      Email:

Password:

Security Question 1:

Security Answer 1:

Security Question 2:

Security Answer 2:

Notes:

**Website:**

Username:                                      Email:

Password:

Security Question 1:

Security Answer 1:

Security Question 2:

Security Answer 2:

Notes:

**Website:**

Username:      Email:

Password:

Security Question 1:

Security Answer 1:

Security Question 2:

Security Answer 2:

Notes:

**Website:**

Username:      Email:

Password:

Security Question 1:

Security Answer 1:

Security Question 2:

Security Answer 2:

Notes:

**Website:**

Username:      Email:

Password:

Security Question 1:

Security Answer 1:

Security Question 2:

Security Answer 2:

Notes:

Website:

Username:        Email:

Password:

Security Question 1:

Security Answer 1:

Security Question 2:

Security Answer 2:

Notes:

Website:

Username:        Email:

Password:

Security Question 1:

Security Answer 1:

Security Question 2:

Security Answer 2:

Notes:

Website:

Username:        Email:

Password:

Security Question 1:

Security Answer 1:

Security Question 2:

Security Answer 2:

Notes:

**Website:**

Username:     Email:

Password:

Security Question 1:

Security Answer 1:

Security Question 2:

Security Answer 2:

Notes:

**Website:**

Username:     Email:

Password:

Security Question 1:

Security Answer 1:

Security Question 2:

Security Answer 2:

Notes:

**Website:**

Username:     Email:

Password:

Security Question 1:

Security Answer 1:

Security Question 2:

Security Answer 2:

Notes:

# F

**Website:**

Username:        Email:

Password:

Security Question 1:

Security Answer 1:

Security Question 2:

Security Answer 2:

Notes:

**Website:**

Username:        Email:

Password:

Security Question 1:

Security Answer 1:

Security Question 2:

Security Answer 2:

Notes:

**Website:**

Username:        Email:

Password:

Security Question 1:

Security Answer 1:

Security Question 2:

Security Answer 2:

Notes:

# G

Website:

Username:                                    Email:

Password:

Security Question 1:

Security Answer 1:

Security Question 2:

Security Answer 2:

Notes:


Website:

Username:                                    Email:

Password:

Security Question 1:

Security Answer 1:

Security Question 2:

Security Answer 2:

Notes:


Website:

Username:                                    Email:

Password:

Security Question 1:

Security Answer 1:

Security Question 2:

Security Answer 2:

Notes:

**G**

**Website:**

Username: ___________________  Email: ___________________

Password: ___________________

Security Question 1: ___________________

Security Answer 1: ___________________

Security Question 2: ___________________

Security Answer 2: ___________________

Notes: ___________________

**Website:**

Username: ___________________  Email: ___________________

Password: ___________________

Security Question 1: ___________________

Security Answer 1: ___________________

Security Question 2: ___________________

Security Answer 2: ___________________

Notes: ___________________

**Website:**

Username: ___________________  Email: ___________________

Password: ___________________

Security Question 1: ___________________

Security Answer 1: ___________________

Security Question 2: ___________________

Security Answer 2: ___________________

Notes: ___________________

**Website:**

Username: | Email:

Password:

Security Question 1:

Security Answer 1:

Security Question 2:

Security Answer 2:

Notes:

**Website:**

Username: | Email:

Password:

Security Question 1:

Security Answer 1:

Security Question 2:

Security Answer 2:

Notes:

**Website:**

Username: | Email:

Password:

Security Question 1:

Security Answer 1:

Security Question 2:

Security Answer 2:

Notes:

**G**

**Website:**

Username: | Email:

Password:

Security Question 1:

Security Answer 1:

Security Question 2:

Security Answer 2:

Notes:

**Website:**

Username: | Email:

Password:

Security Question 1:

Security Answer 1:

Security Question 2:

Security Answer 2:

Notes:

**Website:**

Username: | Email:

Password:

Security Question 1:

Security Answer 1:

Security Question 2:

Security Answer 2:

Notes:

Website:

Username:                                            Email:

Password:

Security Question 1:

Security Answer 1:

Security Question 2:

Security Answer 2:

Notes:


Website:

Username:                                            Email:

Password:

Security Question 1:

Security Answer 1:

Security Question 2:

Security Answer 2:

Notes:


Website:

Username:                                            Email:

Password:

Security Question 1:

Security Answer 1:

Security Question 2:

Security Answer 2:

Notes:

Website:

Username: | Email:

Password:

Security Question 1:

Security Answer 1:

Security Question 2:

Security Answer 2:

Notes:


Website:

Username: | Email:

Password:

Security Question 1:

Security Answer 1:

Security Question 2:

Security Answer 2:

Notes:


Website:

Username: | Email:

Password:

Security Question 1:

Security Answer 1:

Security Question 2:

Security Answer 2:

Notes:

Website:

Username: Email:

Password:

Security Question 1:

Security Answer 1:

Security Question 2:

Security Answer 2:

Notes:

Website:

Username: Email:

Password:

Security Question 1:

Security Answer 1:

Security Question 2:

Security Answer 2:

Notes:

Website:

Username: Email:

Password:

Security Question 1:

Security Answer 1:

Security Question 2:

Security Answer 2:

Notes:

**Website:**

Username:      Email:

Password:

Security Question 1:

Security Answer 1:

Security Question 2:

Security Answer 2:

Notes:

**Website:**

Username:      Email:

Password:

Security Question 1:

Security Answer 1:

Security Question 2:

Security Answer 2:

Notes:

**Website:**

Username:      Email:

Password:

Security Question 1:

Security Answer 1:

Security Question 2:

Security Answer 2:

Notes:

**Website:**

Username:                                        Email:

Password:

Security Question 1:

Security Answer 1:

Security Question 2:

Security Answer 2:

Notes:

**Website:**

Username:                                        Email:

Password:

Security Question 1:

Security Answer 1:

Security Question 2:

Security Answer 2:

Notes:

**Website:**

Username:                                        Email:

Password:

Security Question 1:

Security Answer 1:

Security Question 2:

Security Answer 2:

Notes:

Website:

Username:                                    Email:

Password:

Security Question 1:

Security Answer 1:

Security Question 2:

Security Answer 2:

Notes:


Website:

Username:                                    Email:

Password:

Security Question 1:

Security Answer 1:

Security Question 2:

Security Answer 2:

Notes:


Website:

Username:                                    Email:

Password:

Security Question 1:

Security Answer 1:

Security Question 2:

Security Answer 2:

Notes:

| Website: |
| --- |

Username: ______________________ Email: ______________________

Password: ______________________

Security Question 1: ______________________

Security Answer 1: ______________________

Security Question 2: ______________________

Security Answer 2: ______________________

Notes: ______________________

| Website: |
| --- |

Username: ______________________ Email: ______________________

Password: ______________________

Security Question 1: ______________________

Security Answer 1: ______________________

Security Question 2: ______________________

Security Answer 2: ______________________

Notes: ______________________

| Website: |
| --- |

Username: ______________________ Email: ______________________

Password: ______________________

Security Question 1: ______________________

Security Answer 1: ______________________

Security Question 2: ______________________

Security Answer 2: ______________________

Notes: ______________________

Website:

Username:                                  Email:

Password:

Security Question 1:

Security Answer 1:

Security Question 2:

Security Answer 2:

Notes:


Website:

Username:                                  Email:

Password:

Security Question 1:

Security Answer 1:

Security Question 2:

Security Answer 2:

Notes:


Website:

Username:                                  Email:

Password:

Security Question 1:

Security Answer 1:

Security Question 2:

Security Answer 2:

Notes:

## Website:

| | |
|---|---|
| Username: | Email: |

Password:

Security Question 1:

Security Answer 1:

Security Question 2:

Security Answer 2:

Notes:

## Website:

| | |
|---|---|
| Username: | Email: |

Password:

Security Question 1:

Security Answer 1:

Security Question 2:

Security Answer 2:

Notes:

## Website:

| | |
|---|---|
| Username: | Email: |

Password:

Security Question 1:

Security Answer 1:

Security Question 2:

Security Answer 2:

Notes:

## Website:

Username:                        Email:

Password:

Security Question 1:

Security Answer 1:

Security Question 2:

Security Answer 2:

Notes:

## Website:

Username:                        Email:

Password:

Security Question 1:

Security Answer 1:

Security Question 2:

Security Answer 2:

Notes:

## Website:

Username:                        Email:

Password:

Security Question 1:

Security Answer 1:

Security Question 2:

Security Answer 2:

Notes:

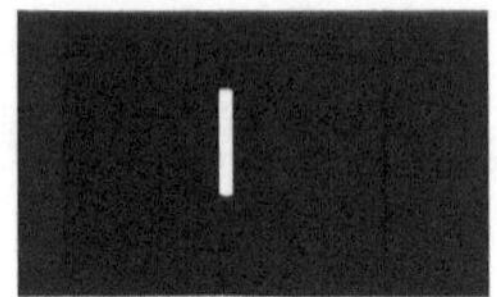

## Website:

Username:            Email:

Password:

Security Question 1:

Security Answer 1:

Security Question 2:

Security Answer 2:

Notes:

## Website:

Username:            Email:

Password:

Security Question 1:

Security Answer 1:

Security Question 2:

Security Answer 2:

Notes:

## Website:

Username:            Email:

Password:

Security Question 1:

Security Answer 1:

Security Question 2:

Security Answer 2:

Notes:

## Website:

| | |
|---|---|
| Username: | Email: |

Password:

Security Question 1:

Security Answer 1:

Security Question 2:

Security Answer 2:

Notes:

## Website:

| | |
|---|---|
| Username: | Email: |

Password:

Security Question 1:

Security Answer 1:

Security Question 2:

Security Answer 2:

Notes:

## Website:

| | |
|---|---|
| Username: | Email: |

Password:

Security Question 1:

Security Answer 1:

Security Question 2:

Security Answer 2:

Notes:

## Website:

Username:          Email:

Password:

Security Question 1:

Security Answer 1:

Security Question 2:

Security Answer 2:

Notes:

## Website:

Username:          Email:

Password:

Security Question 1:

Security Answer 1:

Security Question 2:

Security Answer 2:

Notes:

## Website:

Username:          Email:

Password:

Security Question 1:

Security Answer 1:

Security Question 2:

Security Answer 2:

Notes:

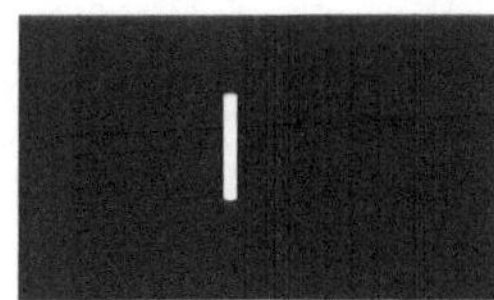

## Website:

Username:                                        Email:

Password:

Security Question 1:

Security Answer 1:

Security Question 2:

Security Answer 2:

Notes:

## Website:

Username:                                        Email:

Password:

Security Question 1:

Security Answer 1:

Security Question 2:

Security Answer 2:

Notes:

## Website:

Username:                                        Email:

Password:

Security Question 1:

Security Answer 1:

Security Question 2:

Security Answer 2:

Notes:

# J

**Website:**

Username:                          Email:

Password:

Security Question 1:

Security Answer 1:

Security Question 2:

Security Answer 2:

Notes:

**Website:**

Username:                          Email:

Password:

Security Question 1:

Security Answer 1:

Security Question 2:

Security Answer 2:

Notes:

**Website:**

Username:                          Email:

Password:

Security Question 1:

Security Answer 1:

Security Question 2:

Security Answer 2:

Notes:

Website:

Username:                                      Email:

Password:

Security Question 1:

Security Answer 1:

Security Question 2:

Security Answer 2:

Notes:

Website:

Username:                                      Email:

Password:

Security Question 1:

Security Answer 1:

Security Question 2:

Security Answer 2:

Notes:

Website:

Username:                                      Email:

Password:

Security Question 1:

Security Answer 1:

Security Question 2:

Security Answer 2:

Notes:

## Website:

**Username:**                    **Email:**

**Password:**

**Security Question 1:**

**Security Answer 1:**

**Security Question 2:**

**Security Answer 2:**

**Notes:**

## Website:

**Username:**                    **Email:**

**Password:**

**Security Question 1:**

**Security Answer 1:**

**Security Question 2:**

**Security Answer 2:**

**Notes:**

## Website:

**Username:**                    **Email:**

**Password:**

**Security Question 1:**

**Security Answer 1:**

**Security Question 2:**

**Security Answer 2:**

**Notes:**

Website:

Username:            Email:

Password:

Security Question 1:

Security Answer 1:

Security Question 2:

Security Answer 2:

Notes:

---

Website:

Username:            Email:

Password:

Security Question 1:

Security Answer 1:

Security Question 2:

Security Answer 2:

Notes:

---

Website:

Username:            Email:

Password:

Security Question 1:

Security Answer 1:

Security Question 2:

Security Answer 2:

Notes:

## Website:

| | |
|---|---|
| Username: | Email: |

Password:

Security Question 1:

Security Answer 1:

Security Question 2:

Security Answer 2:

Notes:

## Website:

| | |
|---|---|
| Username: | Email: |

Password:

Security Question 1:

Security Answer 1:

Security Question 2:

Security Answer 2:

Notes:

## Website:

| | |
|---|---|
| Username: | Email: |

Password:

Security Question 1:

Security Answer 1:

Security Question 2:

Security Answer 2:

Notes:

Website:

Username:                                    Email:

Password:

Security Question 1:

Security Answer 1:

Security Question 2:

Security Answer 2:

Notes:


Website:

Username:                                    Email:

Password:

Security Question 1:

Security Answer 1:

Security Question 2:

Security Answer 2:

Notes:


Website:

Username:                                    Email:

Password:

Security Question 1:

Security Answer 1:

Security Question 2:

Security Answer 2:

Notes:

Website:

Username: ______________________  Email: ______________________

Password:

Security Question 1:

Security Answer 1:

Security Question 2:

Security Answer 2:

Notes:

Website:

Username: ______________________  Email: ______________________

Password:

Security Question 1:

Security Answer 1:

Security Question 2:

Security Answer 2:

Notes:

Website:

Username: ______________________  Email: ______________________

Password:

Security Question 1:

Security Answer 1:

Security Question 2:

Security Answer 2:

Notes:

| Website: |
| --- |

| Username: | Email: |
| --- | --- |

Password:

Security Question 1:

Security Answer 1:

Security Question 2:

Security Answer 2:

Notes:

| Website: |
| --- |

| Username: | Email: |
| --- | --- |

Password:

Security Question 1:

Security Answer 1:

Security Question 2:

Security Answer 2:

Notes:

| Website: |
| --- |

| Username: | Email: |
| --- | --- |

Password:

Security Question 1:

Security Answer 1:

Security Question 2:

Security Answer 2:

Notes:

Website:

Username:                              Email:

Password:

Security Question 1:

Security Answer 1:

Security Question 2:

Security Answer 2:

Notes:

Website:

Username:                              Email:

Password:

Security Question 1:

Security Answer 1:

Security Question 2:

Security Answer 2:

Notes:

Website:

Username:                              Email:

Password:

Security Question 1:

Security Answer 1:

Security Question 2:

Security Answer 2:

Notes:

---

Website:

Username:      Email:

Password:

Security Question 1:

Security Answer 1:

Security Question 2:

Security Answer 2:

Notes:

---

Website:

Username:      Email:

Password:

Security Question 1:

Security Answer 1:

Security Question 2:

Security Answer 2:

Notes:

---

Website:

Username:      Email:

Password:

Security Question 1:

Security Answer 1:

Security Question 2:

Security Answer 2:

Notes:

## Website:

Username:                    Email:

Password:

Security Question 1:

Security Answer 1:

Security Question 2:

Security Answer 2:

Notes:

## Website:

Username:                    Email:

Password:

Security Question 1:

Security Answer 1:

Security Question 2:

Security Answer 2:

Notes:

## Website:

Username:                    Email:

Password:

Security Question 1:

Security Answer 1:

Security Question 2:

Security Answer 2:

Notes:

**Website:**

Username:                                    Email:

Password:

Security Question 1:

Security Answer 1:

Security Question 2:

Security Answer 2:

Notes:

**Website:**

Username:                                    Email:

Password:

Security Question 1:

Security Answer 1:

Security Question 2:

Security Answer 2:

Notes:

**Website:**

Username:                                    Email:

Password:

Security Question 1:

Security Answer 1:

Security Question 2:

Security Answer 2:

Notes:

**Website:**

Username:      Email:

Password:

Security Question 1:

Security Answer 1:

Security Question 2:

Security Answer 2:

Notes:

**Website:**

Username:      Email:

Password:

Security Question 1:

Security Answer 1:

Security Question 2:

Security Answer 2:

Notes:

**Website:**

Username:      Email:

Password:

Security Question 1:

Security Answer 1:

Security Question 2:

Security Answer 2:

Notes:

L



Username:                          Email:

Password:

Security Question 1:

Security Answer 1:

Security Question 2:

Security Answer 2:

Notes:

Website:

Username:                          Email:

Password:

Security Question 1:

Security Answer 1:

Security Question 2:

Security Answer 2:

Notes:

Website:

Username:                          Email:

Password:

Security Question 1:

Security Answer 1:

Security Question 2:

Security Answer 2:

Notes:

| Website: | |
| --- | --- |
| Username: | Email: |
| Password: | |
| Security Question 1: | |
| Security Answer 1: | |
| Security Question 2: | |
| Security Answer 2: | |
| Notes: | |

| Website: | |
| --- | --- |
| Username: | Email: |
| Password: | |
| Security Question 1: | |
| Security Answer 1: | |
| Security Question 2: | |
| Security Answer 2: | |
| Notes: | |

| Website: | |
| --- | --- |
| Username: | Email: |
| Password: | |
| Security Question 1: | |
| Security Answer 1: | |
| Security Question 2: | |
| Security Answer 2: | |
| Notes: | |

**Website:**

Username: | Email:

Password:

Security Question 1:

Security Answer 1:

Security Question 2:

Security Answer 2:

Notes:

---

**Website:**

Username: | Email:

Password:

Security Question 1:

Security Answer 1:

Security Question 2:

Security Answer 2:

Notes:

---

**Website:**

Username: | Email:

Password:

Security Question 1:

Security Answer 1:

Security Question 2:

Security Answer 2:

Notes:

| Website: | |
| --- | --- |
| Username: | Email: |
| Password: | |
| Security Question 1: | |
| Security Answer 1: | |
| Security Question 2: | |
| Security Answer 2: | |
| Notes: | |

| Website: | |
| --- | --- |
| Username: | Email: |
| Password: | |
| Security Question 1: | |
| Security Answer 1: | |
| Security Question 2: | |
| Security Answer 2: | |
| Notes: | |

| Website: | |
| --- | --- |
| Username: | Email: |
| Password: | |
| Security Question 1: | |
| Security Answer 1: | |
| Security Question 2: | |
| Security Answer 2: | |
| Notes: | |

**Website:**

Username:       Email:

Password:

Security Question 1:

Security Answer 1:

Security Question 2:

Security Answer 2:

Notes:


**Website:**

Username:       Email:

Password:

Security Question 1:

Security Answer 1:

Security Question 2:

Security Answer 2:

Notes:


**Website:**

Username:       Email:

Password:

Security Question 1:

Security Answer 1:

Security Question 2:

Security Answer 2:

Notes:

<br>
**M**

| Website: |
| --- |

| Username: | Email: |
| --- | --- |

Password:

Security Question 1:

Security Answer 1:

Security Question 2:

Security Answer 2:

Notes:

| Website: |
| --- |

| Username: | Email: |
| --- | --- |

Password:

Security Question 1:

Security Answer 1:

Security Question 2:

Security Answer 2:

Notes:

| Website: |
| --- |

| Username: | Email: |
| --- | --- |

Password:

Security Question 1:

Security Answer 1:

Security Question 2:

Security Answer 2:

Notes:

Username:                                    Email:

Password:

Security Question 1:

Security Answer 1:

Security Question 2:

Security Answer 2:

Notes:




Username:                                    Email:

Password:

Security Question 1:

Security Answer 1:

Security Question 2:

Security Answer 2:

Notes:




Username:                                    Email:

Password:

Security Question 1:

Security Answer 1:

Security Question 2:

Security Answer 2:

Notes:

**Website:**

Username:                          Email:

Password:

Security Question 1:

Security Answer 1:

Security Question 2:

Security Answer 2:

Notes:

**Website:**

Username:                          Email:

Password:

Security Question 1:

Security Answer 1:

Security Question 2:

Security Answer 2:

Notes:

**Website:**

Username:                          Email:

Password:

Security Question 1:

Security Answer 1:

Security Question 2:

Security Answer 2:

Notes:

Username:      Email:

Password:

Security Question 1:

Security Answer 1:

Security Question 2:

Security Answer 2:

Notes:



Username:      Email:

Password:

Security Question 1:

Security Answer 1:

Security Question 2:

Security Answer 2:

Notes:



Username:      Email:

Password:

Security Question 1:

Security Answer 1:

Security Question 2:

Security Answer 2:

Notes:

Website:

Username:                              Email:

Password:

Security Question 1:

Security Answer 1:

Security Question 2:

Security Answer 2:

Notes:

Website:

Username:                              Email:

Password:

Security Question 1:

Security Answer 1:

Security Question 2:

Security Answer 2:

Notes:

Website:

Username:                              Email:

Password:

Security Question 1:

Security Answer 1:

Security Question 2:

Security Answer 2:

Notes:

| Website: | |
| --- | --- |
| Username: | Email: |
| Password: | |
| Security Question 1: | |
| Security Answer 1: | |
| Security Question 2: | |
| Security Answer 2: | |
| Notes: | |

| Website: | |
| --- | --- |
| Username: | Email: |
| Password: | |
| Security Question 1: | |
| Security Answer 1: | |
| Security Question 2: | |
| Security Answer 2: | |
| Notes: | |

| Website: | |
| --- | --- |
| Username: | Email: |
| Password: | |
| Security Question 1: | |
| Security Answer 1: | |
| Security Question 2: | |
| Security Answer 2: | |
| Notes: | |

Website:

Username:                                    Email:

Password:

Security Question 1:

Security Answer 1:

Security Question 2:

Security Answer 2:

Notes:

Website:

Username:                                    Email:

Password:

Security Question 1:

Security Answer 1:

Security Question 2:

Security Answer 2:

Notes:

Website:

Username:                                    Email:

Password:

Security Question 1:

Security Answer 1:

Security Question 2:

Security Answer 2:

Notes:

**Website:**

Username:        Email:

Password:

Security Question 1:

Security Answer 1:

Security Question 2:

Security Answer 2:

Notes:

**Website:**

Username:        Email:

Password:

Security Question 1:

Security Answer 1:

Security Question 2:

Security Answer 2:

Notes:

**Website:**

Username:        Email:

Password:

Security Question 1:

Security Answer 1:

Security Question 2:

Security Answer 2:

Notes:

Website:

Username:                                        Email:

Password:

Security Question 1:

Security Answer 1:

Security Question 2:

Security Answer 2:

Notes:


Website:

Username:                                        Email:

Password:

Security Question 1:

Security Answer 1:

Security Question 2:

Security Answer 2:

Notes:


Website:

Username:                                        Email:

Password:

Security Question 1:

Security Answer 1:

Security Question 2:

Security Answer 2:

Notes:

N

Website:

Username:                                          Email:

Password:

Security Question 1:

Security Answer 1:

Security Question 2:

Security Answer 2:

Notes:


Website:

Username:                                          Email:

Password:

Security Question 1:

Security Answer 1:

Security Question 2:

Security Answer 2:

Notes:


Website:

Username:                                          Email:

Password:

Security Question 1:

Security Answer 1:

Security Question 2:

Security Answer 2:

Notes:

Website:

Username:　　　　Email:

Password:

Security Question 1:

Security Answer 1:

Security Question 2:

Security Answer 2:

Notes:

---

Website:

Username:　　　　Email:

Password:

Security Question 1:

Security Answer 1:

Security Question 2:

Security Answer 2:

Notes:

---

Website:

Username:　　　　Email:

Password:

Security Question 1:

Security Answer 1:

Security Question 2:

Security Answer 2:

Notes:

Website:

Username:                    Email:

Password:

Security Question 1:

Security Answer 1:

Security Question 2:

Security Answer 2:

Notes:


Website:

Username:                    Email:

Password:

Security Question 1:

Security Answer 1:

Security Question 2:

Security Answer 2:

Notes:


Website:

Username:                    Email:

Password:

Security Question 1:

Security Answer 1:

Security Question 2:

Security Answer 2:

Notes:

Website:

Username:      Email:

Password:

Security Question 1:

Security Answer 1:

Security Question 2:

Security Answer 2:

Notes:


Website:

Username:      Email:

Password:

Security Question 1:

Security Answer 1:

Security Question 2:

Security Answer 2:

Notes:


Website:

Username:      Email:

Password:

Security Question 1:

Security Answer 1:

Security Question 2:

Security Answer 2:

Notes:

## Website:

Username:                          Email:

Password:

Security Question 1:

Security Answer 1:

Security Question 2:

Security Answer 2:

Notes:

## Website:

Username:                          Email:

Password:

Security Question 1:

Security Answer 1:

Security Question 2:

Security Answer 2:

Notes:

## Website:

Username:                          Email:

Password:

Security Question 1:

Security Answer 1:

Security Question 2:

Security Answer 2:

Notes:

**Website:**

Username: Email:

Password:

Security Question 1:

Security Answer 1:

Security Question 2:

Security Answer 2:

Notes:

**Website:**

Username: Email:

Password:

Security Question 1:

Security Answer 1:

Security Question 2:

Security Answer 2:

Notes:

**Website:**

Username: Email:

Password:

Security Question 1:

Security Answer 1:

Security Question 2:

Security Answer 2:

Notes:

## Website:

| | |
|---|---|
| Username: | Email: |

Password:

Security Question 1:

Security Answer 1:

Security Question 2:

Security Answer 2:

Notes:

## Website:

| | |
|---|---|
| Username: | Email: |

Password:

Security Question 1:

Security Answer 1:

Security Question 2:

Security Answer 2:

Notes:

## Website:

| | |
|---|---|
| Username: | Email: |

Password:

Security Question 1:

Security Answer 1:

Security Question 2:

Security Answer 2:

Notes:

| Website: |
| --- |

Username:                                        Email:

Password:

Security Question 1:

Security Answer 1:

Security Question 2:

Security Answer 2:

Notes:

| Website: |
| --- |

Username:                                        Email:

Password:

Security Question 1:

Security Answer 1:

Security Question 2:

Security Answer 2:

Notes:

| Website: |
| --- |

Username:                                        Email:

Password:

Security Question 1:

Security Answer 1:

Security Question 2:

Security Answer 2:

Notes:

Username:                                          Email:

Password:

Security Question 1:

Security Answer 1:

Security Question 2:

Security Answer 2:

Notes:




Username:                                          Email:

Password:

Security Question 1:

Security Answer 1:

Security Question 2:

Security Answer 2:

Notes:




Username:                                          Email:

Password:

Security Question 1:

Security Answer 1:

Security Question 2:

Security Answer 2:

Notes:

# P

Website:

Username: | Email:

Password:

Security Question 1:

Security Answer 1:

Security Question 2:

Security Answer 2:

Notes:

Website:

Username: | Email:

Password:

Security Question 1:

Security Answer 1:

Security Question 2:

Security Answer 2:

Notes:

Website:

Username: | Email:

Password:

Security Question 1:

Security Answer 1:

Security Question 2:

Security Answer 2:

Notes:

## Website:

Username:                              Email:

Password:

Security Question 1:

Security Answer 1:

Security Question 2:

Security Answer 2:

Notes:

## Website:

Username:                              Email:

Password:

Security Question 1:

Security Answer 1:

Security Question 2:

Security Answer 2:

Notes:

## Website:

Username:                              Email:

Password:

Security Question 1:

Security Answer 1:

Security Question 2:

Security Answer 2:

Notes:

**Website:**

Username: | Email:

Password:

Security Question 1:

Security Answer 1:

Security Question 2:

Security Answer 2:

Notes:

**Website:**

Username: | Email:

Password:

Security Question 1:

Security Answer 1:

Security Question 2:

Security Answer 2:

Notes:

**Website:**

Username: | Email:

Password:

Security Question 1:

Security Answer 1:

Security Question 2:

Security Answer 2:

Notes:

**P**

Website:

Username:                              Email:

Password:

Security Question 1:

Security Answer 1:

Security Question 2:

Security Answer 2:

Notes:

Website:

Username:                              Email:

Password:

Security Question 1:

Security Answer 1:

Security Question 2:

Security Answer 2:

Notes:

Website:

Username:                              Email:

Password:

Security Question 1:

Security Answer 1:

Security Question 2:

Security Answer 2:

Notes:

## Website:

Username:                    Email:

Password:

Security Question 1:

Security Answer 1:

Security Question 2:

Security Answer 2:

Notes:

## Website:

Username:                    Email:

Password:

Security Question 1:

Security Answer 1:

Security Question 2:

Security Answer 2:

Notes:

## Website:

Username:                    Email:

Password:

Security Question 1:

Security Answer 1:

Security Question 2:

Security Answer 2:

Notes:

P

Website:

Username:                          Email:

Password:

Security Question 1:

Security Answer 1:

Security Question 2:

Security Answer 2:

Notes:

Website:

Username:                          Email:

Password:

Security Question 1:

Security Answer 1:

Security Question 2:

Security Answer 2:

Notes:

Website:

Username:                          Email:

Password:

Security Question 1:

Security Answer 1:

Security Question 2:

Security Answer 2:

Notes:

| Website: |
| --- |

| Username: | Email: |
| --- | --- |

Password:

Security Question 1:

Security Answer 1:

Security Question 2:

Security Answer 2:

Notes:

| Website: |
| --- |

| Username: | Email: |
| --- | --- |

Password:

Security Question 1:

Security Answer 1:

Security Question 2:

Security Answer 2:

Notes:

| Website: |
| --- |

| Username: | Email: |
| --- | --- |

Password:

Security Question 1:

Security Answer 1:

Security Question 2:

Security Answer 2:

Notes:

**Website:**

Username:          Email:

Password:

Security Question 1:

Security Answer 1:

Security Question 2:

Security Answer 2:

Notes:

**Website:**

Username:          Email:

Password:

Security Question 1:

Security Answer 1:

Security Question 2:

Security Answer 2:

Notes:

**Website:**

Username:          Email:

Password:

Security Question 1:

Security Answer 1:

Security Question 2:

Security Answer 2:

Notes:

## Website:

Username:      Email:

Password:

Security Question 1:

Security Answer 1:

Security Question 2:

Security Answer 2:

Notes:

## Website:

Username:      Email:

Password:

Security Question 1:

Security Answer 1:

Security Question 2:

Security Answer 2:

Notes:

## Website:

Username:      Email:

Password:

Security Question 1:

Security Answer 1:

Security Question 2:

Security Answer 2:

Notes:

**Website:**

Username: | Email:

Password:

Security Question 1:

Security Answer 1:

Security Question 2:

Security Answer 2:

Notes:

---

**Website:**

Username: | Email:

Password:

Security Question 1:

Security Answer 1:

Security Question 2:

Security Answer 2:

Notes:

---

**Website:**

Username: | Email:

Password:

Security Question 1:

Security Answer 1:

Security Question 2:

Security Answer 2:

Notes:

## Website:

Username:                              Email:

Password:

Security Question 1:

Security Answer 1:

Security Question 2:

Security Answer 2:

Notes:

## Website:

Username:                              Email:

Password:

Security Question 1:

Security Answer 1:

Security Question 2:

Security Answer 2:

Notes:

## Website:

Username:                              Email:

Password:

Security Question 1:

Security Answer 1:

Security Question 2:

Security Answer 2:

Notes:

Website:

Username:                                          Email:

Password:

Security Question 1:

Security Answer 1:

Security Question 2:

Security Answer 2:

Notes:


Website:

Username:                                          Email:

Password:

Security Question 1:

Security Answer 1:

Security Question 2:

Security Answer 2:

Notes:


Website:

Username:                                          Email:

Password:

Security Question 1:

Security Answer 1:

Security Question 2:

Security Answer 2:

Notes:

## R

**Website:**

Username:          Email:

Password:

Security Question 1:

Security Answer 1:

Security Question 2:

Security Answer 2:

Notes:

**Website:**

Username:          Email:

Password:

Security Question 1:

Security Answer 1:

Security Question 2:

Security Answer 2:

Notes:

**Website:**

Username:          Email:

Password:

Security Question 1:

Security Answer 1:

Security Question 2:

Security Answer 2:

Notes:

## Website:

Username:      Email:

Password:

Security Question 1:

Security Answer 1:

Security Question 2:

Security Answer 2:

Notes:

## Website:

Username:      Email:

Password:

Security Question 1:

Security Answer 1:

Security Question 2:

Security Answer 2:

Notes:

## Website:

Username:      Email:

Password:

Security Question 1:

Security Answer 1:

Security Question 2:

Security Answer 2:

Notes:

# R

## Website:

Username:                                    Email:

Password:

Security Question 1:

Security Answer 1:

Security Question 2:

Security Answer 2:

Notes:

## Website:

Username:                                    Email:

Password:

Security Question 1:

Security Answer 1:

Security Question 2:

Security Answer 2:

Notes:

## Website:

Username:                                    Email:

Password:

Security Question 1:

Security Answer 1:

Security Question 2:

Security Answer 2:

Notes:

| Website: |
| --- |

| Username: | Email: |
| --- | --- |

Password:

Security Question 1:

Security Answer 1:

Security Question 2:

Security Answer 2:

Notes:

| Website: |
| --- |

| Username: | Email: |
| --- | --- |

Password:

Security Question 1:

Security Answer 1:

Security Question 2:

Security Answer 2:

Notes:

| Website: |
| --- |

| Username: | Email: |
| --- | --- |

Password:

Security Question 1:

Security Answer 1:

Security Question 2:

Security Answer 2:

Notes:

Website:

Username:                                    Email:

Password:

Security Question 1:

Security Answer 1:

Security Question 2:

Security Answer 2:

Notes:

Website:

Username:                                    Email:

Password:

Security Question 1:

Security Answer 1:

Security Question 2:

Security Answer 2:

Notes:

Website:

Username:                                    Email:

Password:

Security Question 1:

Security Answer 1:

Security Question 2:

Security Answer 2:

Notes:

## Website:

Username:                                    Email:

Password:

Security Question 1:

Security Answer 1:

Security Question 2:

Security Answer 2:

Notes:

## Website:

Username:                                    Email:

Password:

Security Question 1:

Security Answer 1:

Security Question 2:

Security Answer 2:

Notes:

## Website:

Username:                                    Email:

Password:

Security Question 1:

Security Answer 1:

Security Question 2:

Security Answer 2:

Notes:

# S

Website:

Username:                              Email:

Password:

Security Question 1:

Security Answer 1:

Security Question 2:

Security Answer 2:

Notes:

Website:

Username:                              Email:

Password:

Security Question 1:

Security Answer 1:

Security Question 2:

Security Answer 2:

Notes:

Website:

Username:                              Email:

Password:

Security Question 1:

Security Answer 1:

Security Question 2:

Security Answer 2:

Notes:

S

Website:

Username:                          Email:

Password:

Security Question 1:

Security Answer 1:

Security Question 2:

Security Answer 2:

Notes:


Website:

Username:                          Email:

Password:

Security Question 1:

Security Answer 1:

Security Question 2:

Security Answer 2:

Notes:


Website:

Username:                          Email:

Password:

Security Question 1:

Security Answer 1:

Security Question 2:

Security Answer 2:

Notes:

# S

Website:

Username:                                   Email:

Password:

Security Question 1:

Security Answer 1:

Security Question 2:

Security Answer 2:

Notes:

Website:

Username:                                   Email:

Password:

Security Question 1:

Security Answer 1:

Security Question 2:

Security Answer 2:

Notes:

Website:

Username:                                   Email:

Password:

Security Question 1:

Security Answer 1:

Security Question 2:

Security Answer 2:

Notes:

**S**

Website:

Username:                                        Email:

Password:

Security Question 1:

Security Answer 1:

Security Question 2:

Security Answer 2:

Notes:


Website:

Username:                                        Email:

Password:

Security Question 1:

Security Answer 1:

Security Question 2:

Security Answer 2:

Notes:


Website:

Username:                                        Email:

Password:

Security Question 1:

Security Answer 1:

Security Question 2:

Security Answer 2:

Notes:

**Website:**

Username:                                        Email:

Password:

Security Question 1:

Security Answer 1:

Security Question 2:

Security Answer 2:

Notes:


**Website:**

Username:                                        Email:

Password:

Security Question 1:

Security Answer 1:

Security Question 2:

Security Answer 2:

Notes:


**Website:**

Username:                                        Email:

Password:

Security Question 1:

Security Answer 1:

Security Question 2:

Security Answer 2:

Notes:

**S**

## Website:

Username:            Email:

Password:

Security Question 1:

Security Answer 1:

Security Question 2:

Security Answer 2:

Notes:

## Website:

Username:            Email:

Password:

Security Question 1:

Security Answer 1:

Security Question 2:

Security Answer 2:

Notes:

## Website:

Username:            Email:

Password:

Security Question 1:

Security Answer 1:

Security Question 2:

Security Answer 2:

Notes:

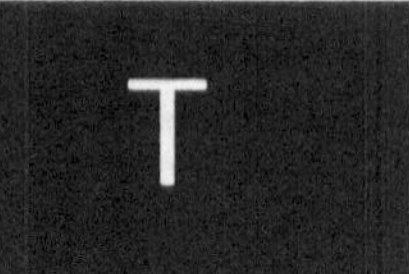



Website:

Username: Email:

Password:

Security Question 1:

Security Answer 1:

Security Question 2:

Security Answer 2:

Notes:

Website:

Username: Email:

Password:

Security Question 1:

Security Answer 1:

Security Question 2:

Security Answer 2:

Notes:

Website:

Username: Email:

Password:

Security Question 1:

Security Answer 1:

Security Question 2:

Security Answer 2:

Notes:

Username:                    Email:

Password:

Security Question 1:

Security Answer 1:

Security Question 2:

Security Answer 2:

Notes:



Username:                    Email:

Password:

Security Question 1:

Security Answer 1:

Security Question 2:

Security Answer 2:

Notes:



Username:                    Email:

Password:

Security Question 1:

Security Answer 1:

Security Question 2:

Security Answer 2:

Notes:

Website:

Username:     Email:

Password:

Security Question 1:

Security Answer 1:

Security Question 2:

Security Answer 2:

Notes:

---

Website:

Username:     Email:

Password:

Security Question 1:

Security Answer 1:

Security Question 2:

Security Answer 2:

Notes:

---

Website:

Username:     Email:

Password:

Security Question 1:

Security Answer 1:

Security Question 2:

Security Answer 2:

Notes:

## Website:

Username:      Email:

Password:

Security Question 1:

Security Answer 1:

Security Question 2:

Security Answer 2:

Notes:

## Website:

Username:      Email:

Password:

Security Question 1:

Security Answer 1:

Security Question 2:

Security Answer 2:

Notes:

## Website:

Username:      Email:

Password:

Security Question 1:

Security Answer 1:

Security Question 2:

Security Answer 2:

Notes:

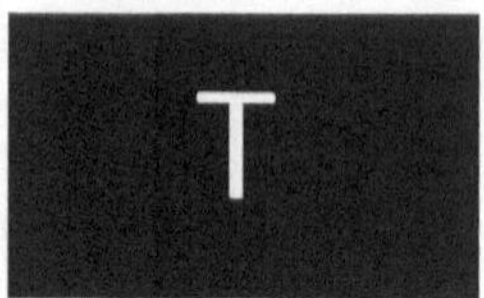



Website:

Username:                                    Email:

Password:

Security Question 1:

Security Answer 1:

Security Question 2:

Security Answer 2:

Notes:


Website:

Username:                                    Email:

Password:

Security Question 1:

Security Answer 1:

Security Question 2:

Security Answer 2:

Notes:


Website:

Username:                                    Email:

Password:

Security Question 1:

Security Answer 1:

Security Question 2:

Security Answer 2:

Notes:

**Website:**

Username:                              Email:

Password:

Security Question 1:

Security Answer 1:

Security Question 2:

Security Answer 2:

Notes:

**Website:**

Username:                              Email:

Password:

Security Question 1:

Security Answer 1:

Security Question 2:

Security Answer 2:

Notes:

**Website:**

Username:                              Email:

Password:

Security Question 1:

Security Answer 1:

Security Question 2:

Security Answer 2:

Notes:

## Website:

Username:      Email:

Password:

Security Question 1:

Security Answer 1:

Security Question 2:

Security Answer 2:

Notes:

## Website:

Username:      Email:

Password:

Security Question 1:

Security Answer 1:

Security Question 2:

Security Answer 2:

Notes:

## Website:

Username:      Email:

Password:

Security Question 1:

Security Answer 1:

Security Question 2:

Security Answer 2:

Notes:

## Website:

Username: | Email:

Password:

Security Question 1:

Security Answer 1:

Security Question 2:

Security Answer 2:

Notes:

## Website:

Username: | Email:

Password:

Security Question 1:

Security Answer 1:

Security Question 2:

Security Answer 2:

Notes:

## Website:

Username: | Email:

Password:

Security Question 1:

Security Answer 1:

Security Question 2:

Security Answer 2:

Notes:

## Website:

Username:                                    Email:

Password:

Security Question 1:

Security Answer 1:

Security Question 2:

Security Answer 2:

Notes:

## Website:

Username:                                    Email:

Password:

Security Question 1:

Security Answer 1:

Security Question 2:

Security Answer 2:

Notes:

## Website:

Username:                                    Email:

Password:

Security Question 1:

Security Answer 1:

Security Question 2:

Security Answer 2:

Notes:

**Website:**

Username:      Email:

Password:

Security Question 1:

Security Answer 1:

Security Question 2:

Security Answer 2:

Notes:

---

**Website:**

Username:      Email:

Password:

Security Question 1:

Security Answer 1:

Security Question 2:

Security Answer 2:

Notes:

---

**Website:**

Username:      Email:

Password:

Security Question 1:

Security Answer 1:

Security Question 2:

Security Answer 2:

Notes:

**Website:**

Username:                                      Email:

Password:

Security Question 1:

Security Answer 1:

Security Question 2:

Security Answer 2:

Notes:

**Website:**

Username:                                      Email:

Password:

Security Question 1:

Security Answer 1:

Security Question 2:

Security Answer 2:

Notes:

**Website:**

Username:                                      Email:

Password:

Security Question 1:

Security Answer 1:

Security Question 2:

Security Answer 2:

Notes:

Website:

Username: Email:

Password:

Security Question 1:

Security Answer 1:

Security Question 2:

Security Answer 2:

Notes:


Website:

Username: Email:

Password:

Security Question 1:

Security Answer 1:

Security Question 2:

Security Answer 2:

Notes:


Website:

Username: Email:

Password:

Security Question 1:

Security Answer 1:

Security Question 2:

Security Answer 2:

Notes:

Website:

Username:                                    Email:

Password:

Security Question 1:

Security Answer 1:

Security Question 2:

Security Answer 2:

Notes:


Website:

Username:                                    Email:

Password:

Security Question 1:

Security Answer 1:

Security Question 2:

Security Answer 2:

Notes:


Website:

Username:                                    Email:

Password:

Security Question 1:

Security Answer 1:

Security Question 2:

Security Answer 2:

Notes:

**Website:**

Username:      Email:

Password:

Security Question 1:

Security Answer 1:

Security Question 2:

Security Answer 2:

Notes:

**Website:**

Username:      Email:

Password:

Security Question 1:

Security Answer 1:

Security Question 2:

Security Answer 2:

Notes:

**Website:**

Username:      Email:

Password:

Security Question 1:

Security Answer 1:

Security Question 2:

Security Answer 2:

Notes:

Website:

Username:                          Email:

Password:

Security Question 1:

Security Answer 1:

Security Question 2:

Security Answer 2:

Notes:


Website:

Username:                          Email:

Password:

Security Question 1:

Security Answer 1:

Security Question 2:

Security Answer 2:

Notes:


Website:

Username:                          Email:

Password:

Security Question 1:

Security Answer 1:

Security Question 2:

Security Answer 2:

Notes:

**Website:**

Username:              Email:

Password:

Security Question 1:

Security Answer 1:

Security Question 2:

Security Answer 2:

Notes:

---

**Website:**

Username:              Email:

Password:

Security Question 1:

Security Answer 1:

Security Question 2:

Security Answer 2:

Notes:

---

**Website:**

Username:              Email:

Password:

Security Question 1:

Security Answer 1:

Security Question 2:

Security Answer 2:

Notes:

Website:

Username:                                    Email:

Password:

Security Question 1:

Security Answer 1:

Security Question 2:

Security Answer 2:

Notes:

Website:

Username:                                    Email:

Password:

Security Question 1:

Security Answer 1:

Security Question 2:

Security Answer 2:

Notes:

Website:

Username:                                    Email:

Password:

Security Question 1:

Security Answer 1:

Security Question 2:

Security Answer 2:

Notes:

**Website:**

Username:                                        Email:

Password:

Security Question 1:

Security Answer 1:

Security Question 2:

Security Answer 2:

Notes:

**Website:**

Username:                                        Email:

Password:

Security Question 1:

Security Answer 1:

Security Question 2:

Security Answer 2:

Notes:

**Website:**

Username:                                        Email:

Password:

Security Question 1:

Security Answer 1:

Security Question 2:

Security Answer 2:

Notes:

## Website:

| | |
|---|---|
| Username: | Email: |

Password:

Security Question 1:

Security Answer 1:

Security Question 2:

Security Answer 2:

Notes:

## Website:

| | |
|---|---|
| Username: | Email: |

Password:

Security Question 1:

Security Answer 1:

Security Question 2:

Security Answer 2:

Notes:

## Website:

| | |
|---|---|
| Username: | Email: |

Password:

Security Question 1:

Security Answer 1:

Security Question 2:

Security Answer 2:

Notes:

Website:

Username:                                    Email:

Password:

Security Question 1:

Security Answer 1:

Security Question 2:

Security Answer 2:

Notes:


Website:

Username:                                    Email:

Password:

Security Question 1:

Security Answer 1:

Security Question 2:

Security Answer 2:

Notes:


Website:

Username:                                    Email:

Password:

Security Question 1:

Security Answer 1:

Security Question 2:

Security Answer 2:

Notes:

**Website:**

Username:      Email:

Password:

Security Question 1:

Security Answer 1:

Security Question 2:

Security Answer 2:

Notes:

**Website:**

Username:      Email:

Password:

Security Question 1:

Security Answer 1:

Security Question 2:

Security Answer 2:

Notes:

**Website:**

Username:      Email:

Password:

Security Question 1:

Security Answer 1:

Security Question 2:

Security Answer 2:

Notes:

**Website:**

Username: ___________  Email: ___________

Password: ___________

Security Question 1: ___________

Security Answer 1: ___________

Security Question 2: ___________

Security Answer 2: ___________

Notes: ___________

**Website:**

Username: ___________  Email: ___________

Password: ___________

Security Question 1: ___________

Security Answer 1: ___________

Security Question 2: ___________

Security Answer 2: ___________

Notes: ___________

**Website:**

Username: ___________  Email: ___________

Password: ___________

Security Question 1: ___________

Security Answer 1: ___________

Security Question 2: ___________

Security Answer 2: ___________

Notes: ___________

Website:

Username:                                     Email:

Password:

Security Question 1:

Security Answer 1:

Security Question 2:

Security Answer 2:

Notes:

Website:

Username:                                     Email:

Password:

Security Question 1:

Security Answer 1:

Security Question 2:

Security Answer 2:

Notes:

Website:

Username:                                     Email:

Password:

Security Question 1:

Security Answer 1:

Security Question 2:

Security Answer 2:

Notes:

Website:

Username:                                          Email:

Password:

Security Question 1:

Security Answer 1:

Security Question 2:

Security Answer 2:

Notes:

Website:

Username:                                          Email:

Password:

Security Question 1:

Security Answer 1:

Security Question 2:

Security Answer 2:

Notes:

Website:

Username:                                          Email:

Password:

Security Question 1:

Security Answer 1:

Security Question 2:

Security Answer 2:

Notes:

| Website: |
| --- |

| Username: | Email: |
| --- | --- |

Password:

Security Question 1:

Security Answer 1:

Security Question 2:

Security Answer 2:

Notes:

| Website: |
| --- |

| Username: | Email: |
| --- | --- |

Password:

Security Question 1:

Security Answer 1:

Security Question 2:

Security Answer 2:

Notes:

| Website: |
| --- |

| Username: | Email: |
| --- | --- |

Password:

Security Question 1:

Security Answer 1:

Security Question 2:

Security Answer 2:

Notes:

**Website:**

Username:      Email:

Password:

Security Question 1:

Security Answer 1:

Security Question 2:

Security Answer 2:

Notes:

---

**Website:**

Username:      Email:

Password:

Security Question 1:

Security Answer 1:

Security Question 2:

Security Answer 2:

Notes:

---

**Website:**

Username:      Email:

Password:

Security Question 1:

Security Answer 1:

Security Question 2:

Security Answer 2:

Notes:

**Website:**

Username:          Email:

Password:

Security Question 1:

Security Answer 1:

Security Question 2:

Security Answer 2:

Notes:

**Website:**

Username:          Email:

Password:

Security Question 1:

Security Answer 1:

Security Question 2:

Security Answer 2:

Notes:

**Website:**

Username:          Email:

Password:

Security Question 1:

Security Answer 1:

Security Question 2:

Security Answer 2:

Notes:

**Website:**

Username: | Email:

Password:

Security Question 1:

Security Answer 1:

Security Question 2:

Security Answer 2:

Notes:


**Website:**

Username: | Email:

Password:

Security Question 1:

Security Answer 1:

Security Question 2:

Security Answer 2:

Notes:


**Website:**

Username: | Email:

Password:

Security Question 1:

Security Answer 1:

Security Question 2:

Security Answer 2:

Notes:

**Website:**

Username:          Email:

Password:

Security Question 1:

Security Answer 1:

Security Question 2:

Security Answer 2:

Notes:

**Website:**

Username:          Email:

Password:

Security Question 1:

Security Answer 1:

Security Question 2:

Security Answer 2:

Notes:

**Website:**

Username:          Email:

Password:

Security Question 1:

Security Answer 1:

Security Question 2:

Security Answer 2:

Notes:

**Website:**

Username: ______________________  Email: ______________________

Password: ______________________

Security Question 1: ______________________

Security Answer 1: ______________________

Security Question 2: ______________________

Security Answer 2: ______________________

Notes: ______________________

**Website:**

Username: ______________________  Email: ______________________

Password: ______________________

Security Question 1: ______________________

Security Answer 1: ______________________

Security Question 2: ______________________

Security Answer 2: ______________________

Notes: ______________________

**Website:**

Username: ______________________  Email: ______________________

Password: ______________________

Security Question 1: ______________________

Security Answer 1: ______________________

Security Question 2: ______________________

Security Answer 2: ______________________

Notes: ______________________

**Website:**

Username:          Email:

Password:

Security Question 1:

Security Answer 1:

Security Question 2:

Security Answer 2:

Notes:

---

**Website:**

Username:          Email:

Password:

Security Question 1:

Security Answer 1:

Security Question 2:

Security Answer 2:

Notes:

---

**Website:**

Username:          Email:

Password:

Security Question 1:

Security Answer 1:

Security Question 2:

Security Answer 2:

Notes:

## Website:

Username:                          Email:

Password:

Security Question 1:

Security Answer 1:

Security Question 2:

Security Answer 2:

Notes:

## Website:

Username:                          Email:

Password:

Security Question 1:

Security Answer 1:

Security Question 2:

Security Answer 2:

Notes:

## Website:

Username:                          Email:

Password:

Security Question 1:

Security Answer 1:

Security Question 2:

Security Answer 2:

Notes:

**Website:**

Username: | Email:

Password:

Security Question 1:

Security Answer 1:

Security Question 2:

Security Answer 2:

Notes:

**Website:**

Username: | Email:

Password:

Security Question 1:

Security Answer 1:

Security Question 2:

Security Answer 2:

Notes:

**Website:**

Username: | Email:

Password:

Security Question 1:

Security Answer 1:

Security Question 2:

Security Answer 2:

Notes:

Website:

Username:                                          Email:

Password:

Security Question 1:

Security Answer 1:

Security Question 2:

Security Answer 2:

Notes:


Website:

Username:                                          Email:

Password:

Security Question 1:

Security Answer 1:

Security Question 2:

Security Answer 2:

Notes:


Website:

Username:                                          Email:

Password:

Security Question 1:

Security Answer 1:

Security Question 2:

Security Answer 2:

Notes:

**Website:**

Username:     Email:

Password:

Security Question 1:

Security Answer 1:

Security Question 2:

Security Answer 2:

Notes:

---

**Website:**

Username:     Email:

Password:

Security Question 1:

Security Answer 1:

Security Question 2:

Security Answer 2:

Notes:

---

**Website:**

Username:     Email:

Password:

Security Question 1:

Security Answer 1:

Security Question 2:

Security Answer 2:

Notes:

Website:

Username:                                    Email:

Password:

Security Question 1:

Security Answer 1:

Security Question 2:

Security Answer 2:

Notes:

Website:

Username:                                    Email:

Password:

Security Question 1:

Security Answer 1:

Security Question 2:

Security Answer 2:

Notes:

Website:

Username:                                    Email:

Password:

Security Question 1:

Security Answer 1:

Security Question 2:

Security Answer 2:

Notes:

# Z

Website:

Username:                                        Email:

Password:

Security Question 1:

Security Answer 1:

Security Question 2:

Security Answer 2:

Notes:

Website:

Username:                                        Email:

Password:

Security Question 1:

Security Answer 1:

Security Question 2:

Security Answer 2:

Notes:

Website:

Username:                                        Email:

Password:

Security Question 1:

Security Answer 1:

Security Question 2:

Security Answer 2:

Notes:

Z

Website:

Username:                                    Email:

Password:

Security Question 1:

Security Answer 1:

Security Question 2:

Security Answer 2:

Notes:


Website:

Username:                                    Email:

Password:

Security Question 1:

Security Answer 1:

Security Question 2:

Security Answer 2:

Notes:


Website:

Username:                                    Email:

Password:

Security Question 1:

Security Answer 1:

Security Question 2:

Security Answer 2:

Notes:

# Z

## Website:

Username:                              Email:

Password:

Security Question 1:

Security Answer 1:

Security Question 2:

Security Answer 2:

Notes:

## Website:

Username:                              Email:

Password:

Security Question 1:

Security Answer 1:

Security Question 2:

Security Answer 2:

Notes:

## Website:

Username:                              Email:

Password:

Security Question 1:

Security Answer 1:

Security Question 2:

Security Answer 2:

Notes:

Website:

Username:                                    Email:

Password:

Security Question 1:

Security Answer 1:

Security Question 2:

Security Answer 2:

Notes:


Website:

Username:                                    Email:

Password:

Security Question 1:

Security Answer 1:

Security Question 2:

Security Answer 2:

Notes:


Website:

Username:                                    Email:

Password:

Security Question 1:

Security Answer 1:

Security Question 2:

Security Answer 2:

Notes:

# Z

Website:

Username:        Email:

Password:

Security Question 1:

Security Answer 1:

Security Question 2:

Security Answer 2:

Notes:

Website:

Username:        Email:

Password:

Security Question 1:

Security Answer 1:

Security Question 2:

Security Answer 2:

Notes:

Website:

Username:        Email:

Password:

Security Question 1:

Security Answer 1:

Security Question 2:

Security Answer 2:

Notes:

**Website:**

Username:          Email:

Password:

Security Question 1:

Security Answer 1:

Security Question 2:

Security Answer 2:

Notes:

---

**Website:**

Username:          Email:

Password:

Security Question 1:

Security Answer 1:

Security Question 2:

Security Answer 2:

Notes:

---

**Website:**

Username:          Email:

Password:

Security Question 1:

Security Answer 1:

Security Question 2:

Security Answer 2:

Notes:

www.ingramcontent.com/pod-product-compliance
Lightning Source LLC
Chambersburg PA
CBHW021404150726

47989CB00005B/2400

*9798600073579*